How Vietnamese Immigrants Made America Home

Coming to America
THE HISTORY OF IMMIGRATION TO THE UNITED STATES

How Vietnamese Immigrants Made America Home

SABINE CHERENFANT

rosen publishing's
rosen central
New York

For my family and for Chet Kozlowski

Published in 2019 by The Rosen Publishing Group, Inc.
29 East 21st Street, New York, NY 10010

Copyright © 2019 by The Rosen Publishing Group, Inc.

First Edition

All rights reserved. No part of this book may be reproduced in any form without permission in writing from the publisher, except by a reviewer.

Library of Congress Cataloging-in-Publication Data

Names: Cherenfant, Sabine, author.
Title: How Vietnamese immigrants made America home / Sabine Cherenfant.
Description: New York : Rosen Central, 2019. | Series: Coming to America: the history of immigration to the United States | Includes bibliographical references and index. | Audience: Grades 5–8.
Identifiers: LCCN 2017044520 | ISBN 9781508181385 (library bound) | ISBN 9781508181392 (pbk.)
Subjects: LCSH: Vietnamese Americans—History—Juvenile literature. | Refugees—Vietnam—History—Juvenile literature. | Refugees—United States—History—Juvenile literature. | Immigrants—United States—History—Juvenile literature. | United States—Emigration and immigration—History—Juvenile literature. | Vietnam—Emigration and immigration—History—Juvenile literature. | Vietnam—History—Juvenile literature.
Classification: LCC E184.V53 C54 2019 | DDC 973/.0495922—dc23
LC record available at https://lccn.loc.gov/2017044520

Manufactured in the United States of America

On the cover: A chef prepares Vietnamese food at The Slanted Door, a restaurant in San Francisco.

CONTENTS

Introduction 6

CHAPTER ONE
A History of Vietnam 10

CHAPTER TWO
War and Refugee Crisis 22

CHAPTER THREE
Moving East: Migration to the United States 38

CHAPTER FOUR
Vietnamese Americans and the Vietnamese Diaspora . . . 51

Fact Sheet 63
Timeline 64
Glossary 66
For More Information 68
For Further Reading 71
Bibliography 72
Index 76

Introduction

Ho Chi Minh, seen here visiting an orphanage in Hanoi, had many pseudonyms, Ho Chi Minh being one of them. He died before the war in Vietnam ended.

INTRODUCTION

Vietnam is a country located in Southeast Asia known for its struggle for independence through the years. It saw the rise and fall of six dynasties and a few regimes. After surviving one thousand years of Chinese occupation, Vietnam became independent of China, and the Vietnamese identity strengthened. Eventually, in 1858, Vietnam fell under the occupation of France and once again saw its identity threatened.

The French occupation lasted close to a century. Vietnamese nationalism remained in place, and after the First Indochina War, Vietnam obtained its independence from France in 1954. The Geneva Accords, which officially removed France's claim over Vietnam, divided the country in two. A zone called the Demilitarized Zone now separated North Vietnam and South Vietnam. That zone was a demilitarized area that in part ran along the Ben Hai River. It offered a few kilometers of space between North and South Vietnam. The Geneva Accords also created the first big Vietnamese migration in modern times as at most eight hundred thousand Vietnamese moved to South Vietnam and approximately one hundred thousand moved to North Vietnam.

North Vietnam was under the leadership of Ho Chi Minh and South Vietnam under the leadership of Ngo Dinh Diem. It was during this time that the United States, motivated by Cold War–era concerns about communism, began interfering in Vietnamese politics by supporting the South Vietnamese government to prevent the spread of communism in Asia. The country was supposed to be reunified two years after the war,

HOW VIETNAMESE IMMIGRANTS MADE AMERICA HOME

but talks between North Vietnam and South Vietnam failed, and the two Vietnamese countries went to war.

Even though the United States was involved in South Vietnamese politics, it officially entered the war in 1964 after the Gulf of Tonkin Incident on August 4 of that year. The war raged for twenty-one years between 1954 and 1975. It resulted in the deaths of millions of Vietnamese, and most of those deaths were civilians. Because of the Rolling Thunder bombing campaign and the spread of toxic herbicides in Vietnam, most of the country's infrastructure and agriculture were damaged. After the fall of Saigon, which officially marked the end of the war, the economy of Vietnam stagnated.

The first refugees of the war were mostly educated Vietnamese who had ties to the United States and could have become targets of the new communist administration. They were evacuated days before the war ended and placed in receiving camps before being resettled in the United States through sponsorships.

Then, a refugee crisis began shortly after the war ended. Thousands of people were leaving Vietnam through unfit boats, and many fell victim to piracy at sea. Many died at sea, but those who survived were placed in camps in different countries before being given asylum in countries like the United States, Canada, Australia and France. They were mostly from rural areas, spoke little English, and made up the second wave of immigrants.

The third wave of immigrants was fewer and part of the Amerasian Homecoming Act, a law that went into effect in

INTRODUCTION

1989. Vietnamese prisoners of war reuniting with family or fleeing Vietnam were also a part of this wave.

Resettling to the United States was not easy. Vietnamese immigrants faced discrimination and the culture shock of a new country. The youth entered a school system that failed to adequately accommodate many the Southeast Asian immigrants. Yet, like all immigrants, Vietnamese immigrants found ways to make the United States home. They created their own communities throughout the United States. Moreover, many notable members of American society are Vietnamese immigrants or descendants of Vietnamese immigrants. Their outlook for the future is bright, but there is still much for the community to overcome.

CHAPTER ONE

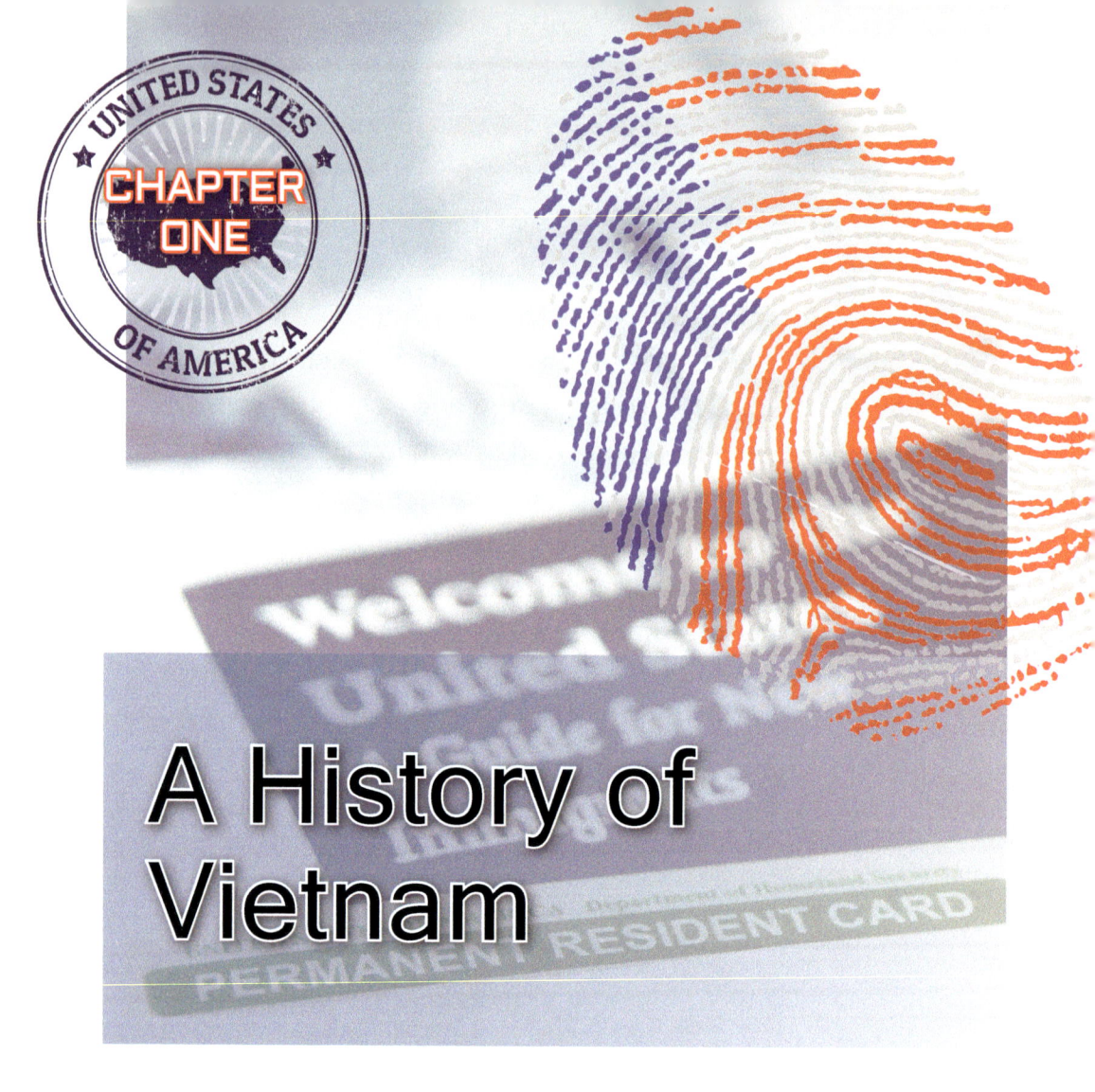

A History of Vietnam

Knowing about the background of Vietnam's domestic and international identity is important for understanding what concerns the Vietnamese have historically had to deal with leading up to immigration to the United States. Vietnam is an ancient civilization that saw its course drastically changed starting with the French occupation in 1858. The end of the French occupation would be the beginning of another contentious period in Vietnamese history.

UNDERSTANDING THE LAND AND THE PEOPLE

Vietnam's land can be divided into three parts: North Vietnam, Central Vietnam, and South Vietnam. The most populous areas are North Vietnam and South Vietnam. Vietnam is mostly an elevated land, and Central Vietnam is composed mostly of mountains.

The legend of Vietnam's origin begins with a union between a dragon and a fairy. Vietnamese civilization began in the Red River Delta at most five thousand years ago. Historians Vu Hong Lien and Peter D. Sharrock describe it as a civilization that spun off from China after one thousand years of Chinese occupation. The Viet, as the people were called, then modified their culture, government structure, writing style, and language.

Most Vietnamese belong to the Kinh ethnic group. Kinh people are indigenous to Vietnam. The Kinh originated in northern Vietnam and southern China. As Kinhs expanded south and took over the Champa Empire along the way, they incorporated other groups, including the Khmer and Cham. Groups mostly located in the northern areas of the country, like the Hmong, migrated from China centuries ago.

Other ethnic groups include the Giay, Muong, Bahnar, Sedang, Katu, Kalo, Cau Ma, Stieng and the Mnong. Some ethnic Chinese groups that made Vietnam home alongside the Kinhs and the others are the Hoa people, the San Diu people, and the Ngai people. There are at least fifty ethnic groups in the country. Most minority ethnic groups live in the mountainous areas of

HOW VIETNAMESE IMMIGRANTS MADE AMERICA HOME

Vietnam maintained close ties to China, its northern neighbor, even as an independent nation. New Vietnamese emperors always sought to be recognized by China.

the country. They are referred to as Vietnamese highlanders because they culturally differ from lowlanders. For example, there are at least twelve other spoken languages in the country besides Vietnamese. The most popular religion in Vietnam is Buddhism, but people there also practice Confucianism, Taoism, Islam, Catholicism, and Caodaism. Although Vietnam has a patriarchal culture, some of the minority groups are matriarchal.

THE RICH CULTURE OF VIETNAM

China and France heavily influenced Vietnam, but Vietnam's own identity as a nation remains vibrant. The culture encompasses all the different ethnic groups of the country. Therefore, the culture itself is heterogeneous, with different languages and different customs. Most Vietnamese live in the countryside and cultivate crops, especially rice, but the urban areas are also heavily populated. Vietnam has a world-renowned cuisine, including the national dish, pho. Rice-based dishes are the most common, and because of the country's proximity to two large rivers and the South China Sea, fish is also a common staple. Soccer is the most popular sport in Vietnam.

HOW VIETNAMESE IMMIGRANTS MADE AMERICA HOME

A CHANGING SOCIETY

Vietnam struggled to remain independent from China. Vu and Sharrock record many revolts during the centuries of Chinese rule, dating back to before the Common Era. Some of these insurgencies, including the rebellion led by the Trung sisters, resulted in temporary sovereignty. Nevertheless, those short bursts of independence always ended with Chinese domination. Consequently, relations between the two countries are important.

Before becoming a concrete independent state with the start of the Ngo dynasty in 939 CE, Vietnamese government consisted of a governor that reported directly to the Chinese emperor. Like China, Vietnam also maintained a monarchy as an independent state, headed by an emperor.

Six dynasties ruled over Vietnam: Ngo dynasty (939–967 CE), Dinh dynasty (968–980), Ly dynasty (1009–1225), Tranh dynasty (1225–1400), Le dynasty (1428–1788), and Nguyen dynasty (1802–1945). Under the Tranh dynasty, Vietnam became the first state to defeat the Mongols in a battle. Official laws of the monarchy reveal the Chinese influences on Vietnamese religion and culture: Buddhism and Confucianism became doctrines for the leadership and the code of behavior in the country. Vietnam also took advantage of its location near the South China Sea to open ports for trade. Those trading activities became the heart of the economy and brought to the Vietnamese doorway traders from Japan, India, Portugal, and the Netherlands.

A HISTORY OF VIETNAM

As the second emperor of the Nguyen dynasty, Minh Mang reigned from 1820 to 1841. This dynasty would become the last Vietnamese dynasty, officially ending in 1945 with Bao Dai.

FRENCH INDOCHINA

During the French occupation, which officially started in 1858, France ended the authority China still maintained over Vietnam. Instead, France became the supreme judge of Vietnamese affairs by requiring French approval for the final decision in appointing new emperors. The new colonial power in Vietnam took over the ports system, imposed new taxes, and appropriated lands of Vietnamese people, especially the highlanders. The French controlled the school system and made French the official language. The French occupation also oversaw the process of legitimizing a romanticized Vietnamese script called *quoc ngu* and started a new class of French-Vietnamese nationals that replaced the existing higher class.

Many Vietnamese never adapted to the French occupation. Nationalist groups and societies emerged at this time, as did a number of political parties, including the Vietnamese Nationalist Party, Indochinese Communist Party, and the New Vietnamese Revolutionary Party. This marked the fall of the emperor-led monarchy.

French colonialism proved to be brutal. The Vietnamese were not treated as equal in their own land. Only a few Vietnamese could receive a higher education, though even those few were not given the same work opportunities as the French. Even more oppressive was the compulsory labor, or corvée, that the French imposed on the Vietnamese.

As part of their occupation, the French forced Vietnamese citizens to strip-mine places like Hon Gai for coal. The corvée imposed on the Vietnamese helped France exploit the mineral resources of Vietnam.

POLITICS POLARIZE VIETNAM

The rise of Ho Chi Minh happened in conjunction with the French losing their grip on Vietnam. Minh took advantage of Germany's invasion of France to return from exile to Vietnam to lead an independence movement. Ho Chi Minh, leader of the Viet Minh (the League for the Independence of Vietnam),

HOW VIETNAMESE IMMIGRANTS MADE AMERICA HOME

Vo Nguyen Giap was instrumental in Vietnam's fight for independence against France. He went on to serve as the defense minister of North Vietnam and helped it seize South Vietnam.

who relied on the military leadership of Vo Nguyen Giap, declared independence from French rule on September 2, 1945, but France refused to cede Indochina as a colony. A series of negotiations with Ho Chi Minh followed. France ultimately proposed to allow Vietnam to govern itself as a member of the French Union. When all negotiations failed, Vietnam and France went into war in a conflict called the First Indochina War.

France enlisted the help of the United States for financial support and weaponry. Even though the United States condemned colonialism, it supported the French fight to recuperate Indochina to prevent the spread of communism. The United States believed that if the Viet Minh won the war and established Vietnam as a communist country, all other countries in Asia would fall to communism and begin to pose a collective threat to the United States. It wasn't until 1954 that the Vietnamese freed themselves of French rule. The Viet Minh won the war in the Battle of Dien Bien Phu by surrounding the French army from the mountains circling the area.

According to Vu Hong Lien and Peter D. Sharrock's in *Descending Dragon, Rising Tiger: A History of Vietnam*, after the Battle of Dien Bien Phu, France and Vietnam signed the Geneva Accords in Geneva, Switzerland. The accords divided the country on opposite sides of a zone called the Vietnamese Demilitarized Zone (DMZ). The Viet Minh and Ho Chi Minh took control of North Vietnam, whereas South Vietnam governed itself. The

HOW VIETNAMESE IMMIGRANTS MADE AMERICA HOME

accord also removed France's authority over Vietnam, Cambodia, and Laos and asked for a truce. In addition, an International Control Committee with Canada, India, and Poland was created to oversee the truce. As part of the agreement, the Vietnamese had three hundred days to move to either North Vietnam or South Vietnam. As many as eight hundred thousand Vietnamese, mostly Catholics, moved to South Vietnam with the help of French aircraft. The number of Viet Minh and citizens that made the move to North Vietnam during that time was one hundred thousand, but they did not receive transportation aid from France or the United States.

South Vietnam saw the rise of Ngo Dinh Diem, who was elected president and subsequently gave administrative titles to friends and family. Bao Dai, the chief of state and former emperor of South Vietnam, was removed during that time in a fraudulent vote. Diem's brother, Ngo Dinh Nhu, became a brutal leader who targeted and victimized Buddhists.

The United States decided to get involved and aid South Vietnam. President Dwight Eisenhower presided over an administration that sought to prevent Vietnam from unifying. When the Geneva Accords asked for a national election to be held two years after the accords were reached, the United States and the anticommunist Vietnamese faction opposed the election because they were certain Ho Chi Minh would win, and Minh's victory would nationalize communism. North Vietnam's economy was crumbling, and the government was already showing signs of authoritarianism because it criminalized the act of opposing the government. North Vietnam reached out to their southern counterpart several times to discuss an election, but the South Vietnamese government never responded.

Vietnam was supposed to be reunified in 1956, two years after the Geneva Accords. Both the United States and the South Vietnam administration opposed it. The election never took place. Instead, hostilities flared into the Second Indochina War. In the United States, the conflict is generally referred to as the Vietnam War.

CHAPTER TWO

War and Refugee Crisis

The Second Indochina War created the largest refugee crisis at its time in Vietnam. Understanding the Vietnamese immigrant journey to the United States begins with understanding the war that the United States instigated.

THE AMERICAN FIGHT AGAINST COMMUNISM

Communism was a political and economic system developed by Karl Marx and Friedrich Engels to offset the economic

WAR AND REFUGEE CRISIS

George Catlett Marshall served as the chief of staff of the US Army during World War II and as secretary of state under President Harry Truman.

struggles of the working class in the 1800s. The system was first adopted in Russia before spreading to different countries in Europe, Asia, Africa, and America. After World War II, the United States began to view communism as a threat to its future and created the Marshall Plan to pump money into Western European countries to prevent them from becoming communist states. The Marshall Plan was named after George Catlett Marshall, the secretary of state under the administration of President Harry Truman. The plan helped sixteen European countries recover after the war, and it helped France pursue its fight to gain Indochina back. In addition, as part of the efforts of the United States to stop communism from expanding, the American army became involved in the Korean War, a conflict that remains unresolved even today.

There was already a communist regime in China, and the United States wanted to contain it. This fight against communism centered in Vietnam after the official collapse of French colonialism. However, it was clearly not in the spirit of allowing self-determined nations to control their destiny.

THE FIRST PHASE OF THE WAR, 1954–1964

The United States provided advisory support to the Ngo Dinh Diem government. The North Vietnamese government therefore viewed South Vietnam as a Western colony because of its attachment to the United States. According to William S. Turley's writing in *The Second Indochina War: A*

The National Liberation Front was North Vietnam's effort in the south to take control of South Vietnam. Although its military arm became known as Viet Cong (Vietnamese Communists), not all members were communists.

Concise Political and Military History, the North Vietnamese government responded by forming its own alliance. It continued to seek support for a reunified Vietnam from Russia and China.

The Geneva Accords guaranteed a period of migration during which the Vietnamese were allowed to move either north or south, but the Viet Minh left behind a number of armed soldiers in South Vietnam—these soldiers made up the National Liberation Front (NLF) and were also known as the Viet Cong. There were also still communications between those soldiers in the south and the Ho Chi Minh government in the north. When it became clear that Vietnam wouldn't be reunified, NLF soldiers reorganized themselves and began a series of small insurgencies that took advantage of the unpopularity of Ngo Dinh Diem.

During this time, the United States and North Vietnam became involved in a supposedly secret civil war in Laos. The Laotian communist regime, Pathet Lao, operated on behalf of one of the main Laotian factions. Thailand also became involved. Moreover, by 1961, three thousand United States military advisors were sent to Saigon. The intention was supposedly for those military advisors to not take part in the fight, but they eventually did. They helped South Vietnam build a stronger military to counter the strong hand that the communist guerrilla forces had in the south.

Those who fought for the reunification of Vietnam indeed possessed a sophisticated military and transportation system that went through Cambodia and Laos. This transport system was dubbed the Ho Chi Minh Trail.

Following the Buddhist uprising and the growing hostility of South Vietnamese people toward Ngo Dinh Diem and his brother Ngo Dinh Nhu, the United States decided that it would be in its best interest to forcefully remove Ngo Dinh Diem and his brother in a coup. There is no evidence that the United States stayed involved in the coup until the end, but on November 2, 1963, Ngo Dinh Diem and Ngo Dinh Nhu were murdered.

THE SECOND PHASE OF THE WAR, 1965–1968

The Gulf of Tonkin attack on August 2, 1964, led to the second phase of the war. This event is also known as the Gulf of Tonkin Incident. The *Maddox*, an American destroyer, was stationed in the Gulf of Tonkin, 4 miles (6.4 kilometers) away from North Vietnamese territory in an area the Americans claimed was international waters. The destroyer was there to spy on North Vietnamese activities. The North Vietnamese army attacked the *Maddox* on August 2, and because the American navy believed that North Vietnam was going to attack the *Maddox* again on August 4, President Lyndon B. Johnson decided to attack North Vietnam by air. On August 7, Congress passed the Gulf of Tonkin Resolution, giving the president broad war powers. It wasn't a declaration of war, but it did authorize the United States to take part in activities common to war. Now, the United States officially took over South Vietnam's role in the war in a strategy called the Americanization of the war.

The first Marines arrived in March 1965. American military efforts consisted of strafing the north from that time until the end of October 1968. This military operation was known as Rolling Thunder, and the objective of those airstrikes was to destroy key places in order to hinder North Vietnamese

HOW VIETNAMESE IMMIGRANTS MADE AMERICA HOME

General William Westmoreland led the US military efforts in Vietnam from 1964 to 1968. The legacy of his war strategies, including Search and Destroy, is still debatable.

resistance efforts. During this time, it is estimated that more than 643,000 tons (583,320 metric tons) of bombs were dropped on North Vietnam.

Both China and Russia sent support to North Vietnam to counteract the United States. In addition to sending supplies to North Vietnam between 1956 and 1963, China sent its own military manpower in 1964 to protect the north side of the country while the North Vietnamese army was sent to fight in the south. The United States also demanded support from other countries, including France and Britain. New Zealand, Thailand, the Philippines, South Korea, and Australia joined forces with the United States, but Americans contributed the most to the war effort. The involvement of so many powers helped to define the war as a collective fight for freedom, as opposed to an American war. Even as the war began to take a new shape, however, the origins of the conflict never eluded the Vietnamese or the Americans.

What anticommunist forces did find elusive was the ability to counteract the guerrilla style of fighting. Journalist and Vietnam veteran Philip Caputo explains in his book *10,000 Days of Thunder* that "the Viet Cong seldom wore uniforms. A rice-paddy farmer plowing his field behind a water buffalo was [just as] likely to be a guerrilla fighter as not."

Lieutenant General William C. Westmoreland was charged with leading the American war strategy. His strategy consisted of weakening the enemy by destroying the dense woodland with herbicide. The strategy also included bombing areas where they believed the enemy hid. This strategy, known as Search and Destroy, could not adequately take into account the difficulty of telling combatants from civilians. Various incidents demonstrated that the American forces weren't too particular about targeting only combatants. The war resulted in millions of civilian deaths, as well as incidents of mass murder. One incident of mass murder that American forces committed occurred on March 16, 1968. American soldiers killed three hundred civilians, including children, in My Lai, South Vietnam.

THE THIRD AND FINAL PHASE OF THE WAR, 1969–1975

Slightly before My Lai, the National Liberation Front decided to change their strategy. One of the key battles of the conflict took place in Saigon and Hue on January 30, 1968. It is remembered as the beginning of the Tet Offensive because it began during the Tet, or New Year, holiday. It marked the first time Saigon was attacked, and it was televised in the United States. Thousands of civilians died, and ancient buildings including the Hue imperial palace buildings, the Nguyen dynasty tombs, and the Cham monuments of Dong Duong and My Son were destroyed.

Another impact of the Tet Offensive was that Americans lost confidence in their standing in the war. The NLF's Tet Offensive strategy failed, but this event marked the point at which American opposition to involvement in the Vietnam War peaked.

WAR AND REFUGEE CRISIS

Growing criticism led President Johnson to end his presidency after one term. On May 10, 1968, the United States and North Vietnam started to discuss a cease-fire in Paris. In addition, on November 1, 1968, President Johnson ended Operation Rolling Thunder.

When President Richard Nixon took office in 1969, he established a new policy to Vietnamize the war, or shift

> On May 2, 1975, the square in front of the opera house in Hanoi was crowded with a victory march that included military officers.

control and responsibility for defeating the NLF to the South Vietnamese. After the Tet Offensive, the South Vietnamese army strengthened, and the number of American soldiers in Vietnam began to decline. As the American army decreased its manpower, it allocated all its military supplies and gear to the South Vietnamese army. The United States then changed its effort, dropping the Search and Destroy operation to focus on developing South Vietnam as a politically sustainable country.

President Nixon's plan was to expedite the Vietnamization process. When the talks resulted again in a stalemate, President Nixon shelled Hanoi for twelve days in a Christmas bombing operation that resulted in permanent damage to North Vietnam's infrastructure, the deaths of 2,380 Vietnamese, and more than 1,000 wounded people. By 1970, the war had already spread to neighboring countries Laos and Cambodia. Congress ended the Gulf of Tonkin Resolution and restrained American support of South Vietnam.

After the Christmas bombing, all parties signed a truce, but the war went on without the United States. After sixty days, US forces completely left Vietnam. With the United States out of the picture, North Vietnam resumed its plan to reunify the country. The war intensified in March, and North Vietnam gained the advantage. Pleiku and Kon Tum, in the highland region, became so dangerous so that four hundred thousand inhabitants fled. Many died trying to escape. On April 30, 1975, the North Vietnamese troops took Saigon, and the South Vietnamese government abdicated. The war was finally over.

THE AMERASIANS

Many children of Vietnamese women and American soldiers were born during the war. There is no official number as to how many Amerasians were born during that time, but most migrated to the United States during the third wave of Vietnamese immigration. They were a reminder of the American interference. They suffered discrimination and alienation in Vietnam. Many were raised in orphanages, and even though most now live in the United States, only about 3 percent met their American fathers. Initially, before the American government agreed to bring them to the United States in Operation Babylift and later as part of the Amerasian Homecoming Act, they were ignored. Many were bullied in school and became homeless in the streets of South Vietnam.

EVACUATION AND CASUALTIES

More than 58,000 Americans died in the war and 153,000 were wounded. One million Vietnamese soldiers and four million civilians died. When the United States realized that South Vietnam would lose, expats and South Vietnamese

HOW VIETNAMESE IMMIGRANTS MADE AMERICA HOME

with ties to the United States evacuated to the United States. The first evacuation effort, Operation Babylift, took place on April 2, 1975. It consisted of bringing to the United States South Vietnamese children who lost their parents during the war. Of the children in this operation, 2,700 were orphans evacuated to the United States, and several of them were children fathered by American soldiers. During Operation Babylift, 133 children, 33 adults, and 11 military staff died in a plane crash. The day before the war officially ended, American troops made one last evacuation effort, in a procedure called Operation Freewind. By the end of the effort, more than 3,000 Americans, South Vietnamese, and other foreign nationals had been evacuated. Another 400 people trying to escape were left behind at the embassy.

WAR AND REFUGEE CRISIS

The war displaced more than one million Vietnamese. Some immigrants, including those shown here, took shelter in Canada, which now has the third-largest population from the Vietnamese diaspora.

THE FIRST-WAVE IMMIGRANTS

By the time the war ended, the United States had another new president. Richard Nixon had resigned after the Watergate scandal in 1974 and ceded his position to Gerald Ford. President Ford authorized the attorney general to use his "parole power" to admit 130,000 refugees into the United States on March 18, 1975. This power was granted to the attorney general as part of the McCarran-Walter Act, and it gave the attorney general the authority to allow immigrants into the United States in case of emergency.

Monique Avakian notes in *Atlas of Asian-American History* that the McCarran-Walter Act was enacted to discriminate against Asian Americans because it also gives the attorney general the authority to revert immigrants' legal right to stay in the country if they are suspected of communist ties. Avakian also mentions that the act additionally placed a ceiling on the number of Asian immigrants allowed to come into the country while not limiting European immigration. Avakian goes on to describe how the American government first only planned to fetch seventeen thousand "US employees and their families," but eventually admitted to the evacuation "Vietnamese employees and those whose lives were immediately threatened by the change in power."

WAR AND REFUGEE CRISIS

The first wave of immigrants consisted mainly of South Vietnamese professionals, members of the educated class, and South Vietnamese governmental and military personnel. Most of them were Catholics and knowledgeable in English. Because the American-Vietnam war also affected Cambodia and Laos, 5 percent of the 130,000 refugees were Cambodians.

The number of refugees who came to the United States under this program ultimately surpassed the quota as more and more people fled. Some of the first-wave immigrants included journalist Anh Do, who was a child at the time. Do wrote about her experiences in "Vietnamese Refugees Began New Lives in Camp Pendleton's 1975 'Tent City.'" She also writes of factory owner Tuan Lam, who provided military gear and food to the American troops. Lam is the brother of Tony Lam, the first Vietnamese American elected to political office in the United States.

CHAPTER THREE

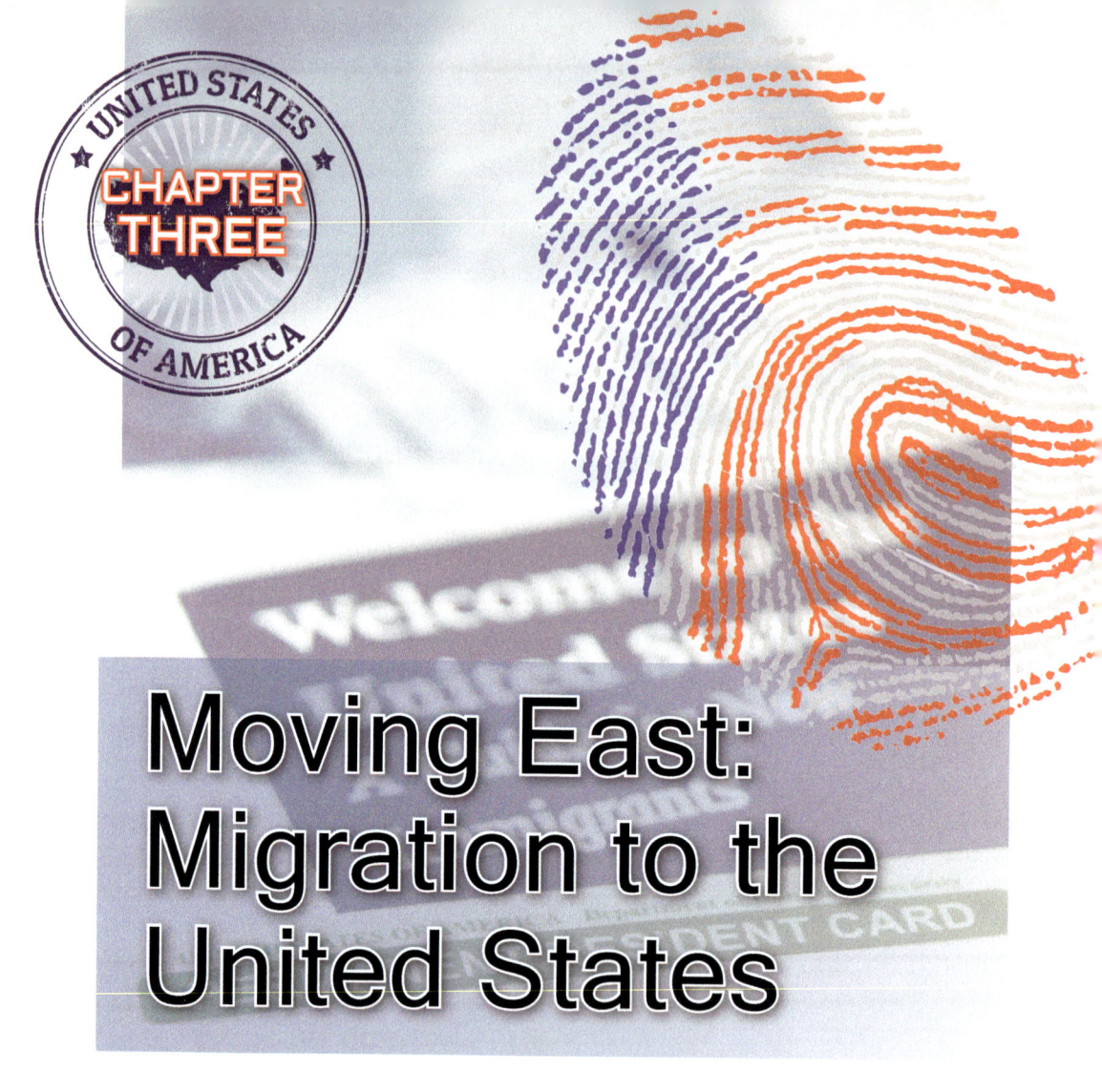

Moving East: Migration to the United States

Vietnamese people came to the United States in three waves, and each wave brought members of a different demographic. By 1965, US immigration laws had become flexible enough to allow non-European immigrants into the country. New laws and measures helped alleviate the various Asian refugee crises of the late twentieth century.

MOVING EAST: MIGRATION TO THE UNITED STATES

RESETTLEMENT EFFORTS IN THE UNITED STATES

Most of the evacuees immediately following the end of the Vietnam War were temporarily placed in a US military base in Guam, a US territory in the Pacific Ocean, to be processed. Four stations were set up to attend to the needs of the refugees as they awaited sponsorship. Those four camps in California,

Guam was the primary evacuation center at the end of the war in Vietnam. On April 26, 1975, four days before the fall of Saigon, Vietnamese evacuees wait in a long line for food at Tin City in Guam.

Florida, Pennsylvania, and Arkansas were respectively Camp Pendleton, Eglin Air Force Base, Fort Indiantown Gap, and Fort Chaffee. Camp Pendleton, a military base located in Southern California, received fifty thousand of these refugees. This was the highest number of refugees at any of the camps. A lot of these refugees settled in the area permanently, so this so-called tent city helped restructure the demographics of Southern California.

When the evacuees first arrived at the camp, they were vaccinated and given a hygienic kit that consisted of a washcloth and toothpaste. Because they were not accustomed to the chilly weather, they were also given military jackets that were too big for many, especially the children. Loc Nam Nguyen, a former refugee at Camp Pendleton, explained to *Los Angeles Times* reporter My-Thuan Tran that the tent city was communal, and he lived with forty other refugees in the shelter where he slept and shared a public bathroom with the other refugees. To help the refugees adjust to the temporary relocation center, the American military engaged local volunteers for kid-friendly activities and other entertainment. The hardest part of living in the tent city was figuring out how to rebuild life in a new country. According to Ahn Do, life in Pendleton was full of uncertainty.

To help relocate the evacuees, the US Office of Refugee Resettlement engaged nine voluntary services (VOLAG), including religious groups, to help the refugees find sponsors and assimilate to the United States. Those voluntary agencies consisted of the United States Catholic Conference, the Lutheran Immigration and Refugee Service, the International

Rescue Committee, the United Hebrew Immigrant Aid Society, World Church Service, the Tolstoy Foundation, the American Fund for Czechoslovak Refugees, the American Council for Nationalities Services, and Traveler's Aid-International Social Services. According to Sucheng Chan, those organizations received a $500 fund per refugee from the federal government. The United States Catholic Conference was the most prominent service because most of the first-wave immigrants were Catholics.

The sponsors were tasked with providing housing, clothing, and support for job searches, as well as with helping the refugees register their children in public schools. VOLAG helped resettle 121,610 refugees from the first wave of immigration. But Americans were generally hostile to the refugees, and it was difficult to find sponsors. Consequently, many refugees remained in the tent cities for an extended period. All the tent cities eventually dissolved in December 1975.

VIETNAM UNDER COMMUNIST RULE

After North Vietnam conquered South Vietnam, it unified and renamed the country the Socialist Republic of Vietnam. Moreover, as punishment for supporting the war against North Vietnam, one million South Vietnamese were sent to reeducation centers, where they spent days or weeks. Those who were part of the South Vietnamese government and military became prisoners in labor camps, where they stayed

HOW VIETNAMESE IMMIGRANTS MADE AMERICA HOME

for at least ten years. Many died in those labor camps, and others became impaired.

The war destroyed the country. During the war, the United States used a toxic chemical called Agent Orange as an herbicide. It was spread over 6 million acres (2.4 million hectares) of land in Vietnam. Not only did Agent Orange cause birth defects in children born to those who had been exposed to it and other health issues for Vietnamese and American soldiers, it also devastated the agriculture of Vietnam. This, coupled with

Bien Hoa Air Base was used by both the American and South Vietnamese military. Because of Operation Ranch Hand, the US defoliation program in Vietnam, dioxins from Agent Orange are heavily concentrated there.

the reduced foreign funding from the United States and China for North Vietnam, resulted in a period of economic stillness. The new government decided to mend the economic deficit by forcing masses of Vietnamese to go back to the rural area to develop the agriculture. The government also created new economic zones, which consisted of dreadful labor that caused the deaths of many.

The new government also focused on removing the class system. This process, which affected mostly Hoa people, consisted of seizing private property and harassing those who were of Chinese descent. In addition, in 1979, Vietnam launched an attack on Cambodia to remove a pro-Chinese government, which drove China to invade Vietnam again. Those calamities exhausted the country and created the second wave of immigrants.

THE SECOND-WAVE IMMIGRANTS

Many refugees of the wave that began in 1979 were Hoa people who fled the country because of persecution. The new communist regime also expelled many from the country. Approximately 250,000 Vietnamese people resettled in China, but most of the 800,000 who left during the two decades after the Vietnam War ended took to the sea and became so-called boat people.

The travel at sea was dangerous. There were often too many people packed in boats that were unfit for the trip. At

The Vietnamese refugee crisis was marked by people taking to sea to escape their war-torn country. Many perished, but approximately eight hundred thousand people between 1975 and 1995 successfully relocated.

sea, they became targets of Thai pirates, who sexually harassed and murdered the refugees. Moreover, thousands died at sea by drowning, starving, or succumbing to illnesses. Their destination was also uncertain because many countries and territories denied them entry. The refugees were ultimately accepted in camps in Thailand, Malaysia, the Philippines, and Hong Kong.

The refugees in the second wave differed from the first wave in that most of them came from the rural class and were much less educated. According to Chan, the second-wave immigrants were also comprised of members of the Hmong ethnic group, who helped the Americans during the war and became subject to punishment from North Vietnam. Other ethnic groups were part of the second wave. Moreover, this wave consisted of fewer

MOVING EAST: MIGRATION TO THE UNITED STATES

Catholics and more Buddhists and animists. The refugee crisis also included evacuees from Cambodia and Laos.

Refugees sometimes stayed in camps for months. Other times, those who survived the trip at sea were forced to remain in the vessel that carried them until they could be admitted to a country. Many ended up resettling in the United States. By mid-1979, two hundred thousand Vietnamese immigrants resettled there. Others ended up settling in Canada, Australia, and France.

TESTIMONIES OF A VIETNAMESE AMERICAN

In 1999, Andrew X. Pham published a memoir called *Catfish and Mandala*. It depicts his struggle as a Vietnamese American. The book went on to win the Kiriyama Pacific Rim Book Prize. In his book, he covers the struggle to both assimilate to the United States and reconnect to Vietnam as he journeys through Vietnam on his bicycle. Pham also demonstrates through personal tales the rough edges of finding one's identity. Pham writes, "We return [as tourists to Vietnam], with our hearts in our throats, to taunt the Communist regime … Mostly, we return because we are lost."

LAWS IN SUPPORT OF THE REFUGEE CRISIS

In 1965, the United States rectified its immigration policy so that it would be easier for immigrants from Asian countries to come to the United States. The Immigration and Nationality Act of 1965, also called the Hart-Celler Act, after Senator Philip Hart and Representative Emanuel Celler, rid the country's immigration policy of its "national origins" language. The US government didn't anticipate the great inflow of Asian immigrants that followed. In her book *Asian Americans: An Interpretive History* Sucheng Chan writes, "The proponents of the act … anticipated … that there would be only a slight increase in Asian immigration because they thought there were too few citizens of Asian ancestry in the country." According to Chan, the change in immigration was also a way for the United States to improve its civil rights image.

The McCarran-Walter Act of 1952 was instrumental in initially allowing Vietnamese evacuees to enter the United States as parolees. The United States also established the Indochina Migration and Refugee Assistance Act in 1975 to compensate state governments for the financial assistance provided to refugees. The government also contributed financially to places that offered English tutoring, employment assistance, and therapy to the refugees. As stated by Chan, "The government also tried to minimize the financial burden on any single locality by dispersing the refugees widely."

Senator Philip Hart (*shown here*), along with Representative Emanuel Celler, proposed the Hart-Celler Immigration and Nationality Act of 1965, removing the racial component of American immigration policies.

The United States devoted about $11 billion to the refugee crisis from 1975 to 1992. To help refugees emigrate from Vietnam and other neighboring Southeast Asian countries to the United States, the federal government established three initiatives during that time: the Special Parole Program of 1975, the Indochinese Parole Programs that lasted from 1977 to 1980, and the Refugee Act of 1980. In total, those programs facilitated the transition of 1,427,846 Southeast Asian refugees into the United States. The Refugee Act of 1980 was particularly important, as 72 percent of the refugees came under terms established by this act.

The Refugee Act of 1980 limited the number of refugees the United States would accept every year to fifty thousand, although the president of the United States had the power to authorize more refugees than the quota allowed. The Office of the United Nations High Commissioner for Refugees (UNHCR) led the international resettlement efforts. The international resettlement efforts were divided into two parts: first-asylum countries that temporarily lodged the refugees in the Southeast Asian region and second-asylum countries where the refugees permanently resettled.

Canada, which according to the Migration Policy Institute is the third-largest residence of the Vietnamese diaspora, approved an immigration act in 1978 to accommodate the admission of Vietnamese refugees. Before the NLF overtook South Vietnam, Canada had already granted entry to fourteen thousand South Vietnamese with family in Canada who wished to leave their home country. Canada extended this by giving permanent resident status to four thousand Vietnamese immigrants in Canada. Even though the act of 1978 asked that refugees be familiar with the two main languages spoken in Canada or have a "desirable profession or trade," immigration to Canada proved to be flexible. The Canadian government called on citizens, religious groups, and other organizations

The war orphaned many children. Vietnamese orphanages like the Bamboo Shoot Orphanage sheltered them, along with Amerasians. Moreover, many children were born with birth defects because of Agent Orange.

to sponsor refugees and promised to sponsor a corresponding number of refugees. The result was that the refugee crisis changed the demographics of Canadian immigrants. According to a CBC Radio article called "The Vietnam War: Canada's Role, Part Two: The Boat People," Vietnamese people accounted for 25 percent of Canadian immigrants between 1978 and 1981.

THE THIRD-WAVE IMMIGRANTS

According to a 2014 Migration Policy Institute article by Jeanne Batalova and Hataipreuk Rkasnuam, the third wave of refugees came in the 1980s and 1990s. This was the smallest wave. It included the Vietnamese Amerasians and political prisoners. The Amerasian Homecoming Act was passed in 1987 to allow forty-six thousand children of American fathers to come to the United States with their families. Batalova and Rkasnuam's article explains that those forty-six thousand children had to be "born between January 1, 1962, and January 1, 1977." By 2000, Batalova and Rkasnuam estimate, the Vietnamese immigrant population in the United States had risen to 988,000.

CHAPTER FOUR

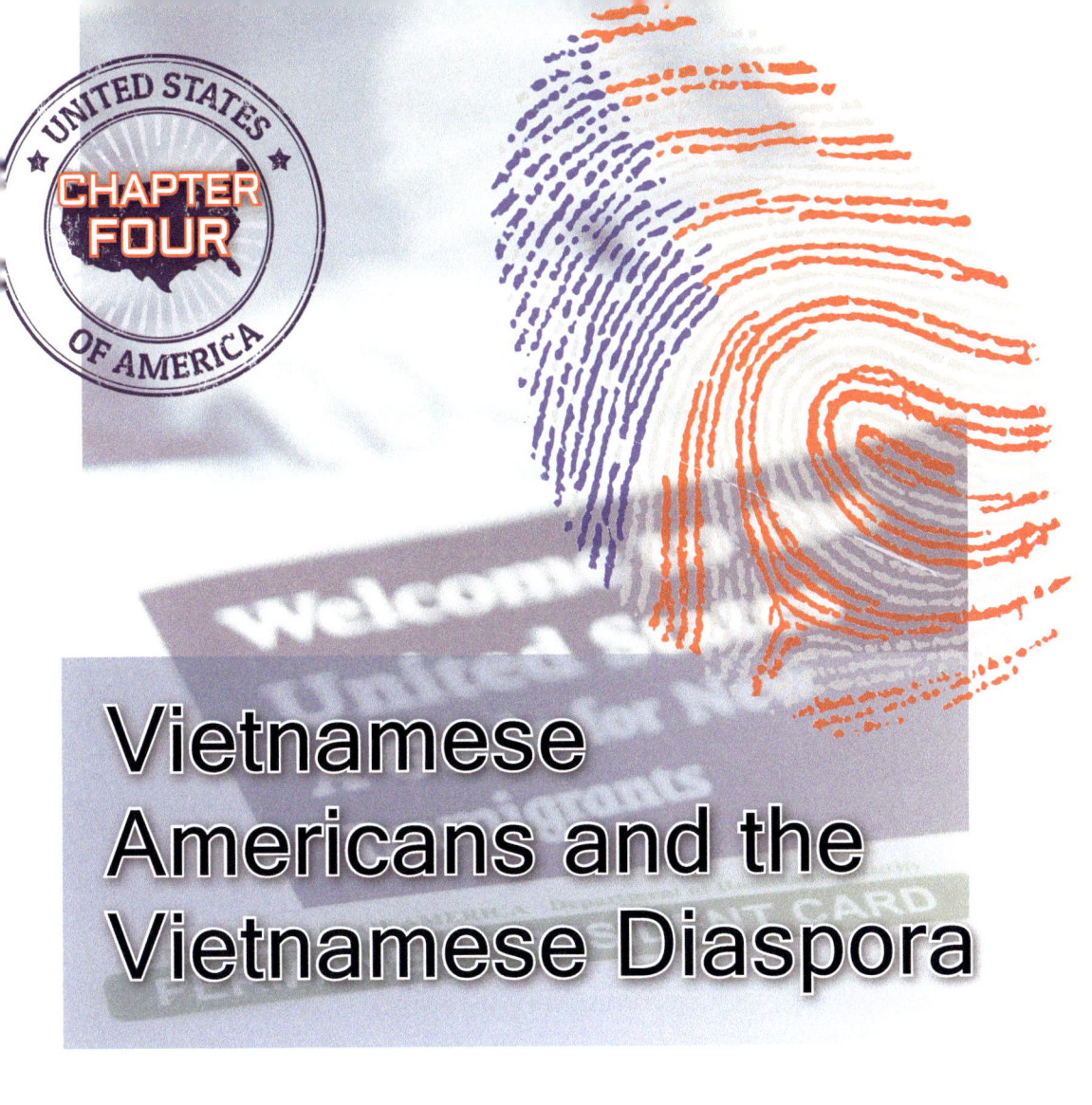

Vietnamese Americans and the Vietnamese Diaspora

Coming to the United States was not easy for Vietnamese immigrants. Vietnamese immigrants suffered racism and alienation because of American sentiment against the war. Many Americans considered Vietnamese immigrants to be the enemy. Still, Vietnamese Americans are part of the fabric of the United States and have contributed much since they first arrived.

EARLY ECONOMIC MAKEUP

The social-class status of most Vietnamese who moved to the United States varies depending on when they migrated. Because the first-wave immigrants of 1975 were more educated and had been settled in the United States for longer, in 1988, their annual income was higher than the annual income of the second-wave immigrants. The 1988 annual income for those first-wave immigrants was $13,000.00, or $27,586.40 when adjusted for inflation to August 2017 monetary values. In 2012, the median income rose to $55,736.00, or $60,372.12 when adjusted for inflation to August 2017 monetary values.

According to Dr. Phitsamay Uy, who advocates for the needs of Southeast Asian American students and codirects the Center for Asian American Studies at the University of Massachusetts-Lowell, it is important to examine those numbers with family makeup in mind. Even though the median annual income for Vietnamese immigrants is higher than the national average, it does not automatically reflect the number of family members per household. Oftentimes, Vietnamese American households tend to be multigenerational.

According to Linda Perrin's book *Coming to America: Immigrants from the Far East*, the language barrier was one of the biggest and most common issues impacting Vietnamese Americans. It often forced Vietnamese professionals to take jobs below their abilities.

Ethnic enclaves, like Little Saigon in Westminster, California, are important to immigrants because they help them create a social network and find support in adapting to the United States.

Vietnamese immigrants also dealt with feeling isolated. They decided to move to areas where there were more Vietnamese people. A sizeable migration to California, Texas, and Louisiana created various community clusters there. For example, in the 1980s, a segment of Bolsa Avenue in Westminster, California, was officially labeled "Little Saigon" because it housed so many

Vietnamese businesses. This way of settling was known as secondary migration because it involved moving to another location after finding a home outside of the tent cities.

Dr. Uy explained in a 2017 interview, "Those communities create a social network structure within their ethnic enclaves." There, Vietnamese immigrants could fulfill all their economic needs in Vietnamese.

VIETNAMESE CHILDREN IN AMERICAN SCHOOLS

Vietnamese became among the top five most spoken languages among English language learners (ELLs) in US schools. In fact, one in two Vietnamese people in the United States did not speak English well. Many Vietnamese people heard Vietnamese at home and English in school.

Dr. Uy explained that school was especially difficult. Very few Vietnamese students were integrated in the American school system. Many students were misdiagnosed with learning disabilities because of their lack of English language skills. The students' silence and lack of attempt at communicating led teachers to assume that their Vietnamese students had mental or physical disabilities. Many were referred to special education programs. Students who witnessed war may have in fact been suffering from post-traumatic stress disorder (PTSD), which could have contributed to their silence. Many children who witness war and trauma suffer from PTSD decades after the fact.

Two Vietnamese students are pictured here in 1980 at the Samuel Chase Elementary School in Maryland. Schools were often unprepared for the needs of the children of Vietnamese immigrants.

A CONTEMPORARY LOOK AT VIETNAMESE AMERICANS

About 40 percent of Vietnamese immigrants live in California. Orange County, Los Angeles County, and Santa Clara County account for 26 percent of the Vietnamese immigrants in the United States. Orange County is indeed the county with the greatest concentration of Vietnamese immigrants. It includes Westminster, where Little Saigon is located. According to a 2014 *Los Angeles Times* article by Anh Do and Christopher Goffard, Orange County was a predominantly white area prior to 2003. It became home to a population with a diverse ethnic background, including Chinese, Korean, and Japanese people. Do and Goffard's article points out that 41 percent of the population in Orange County is Asian American. In

A VILLAGE CALLED VERSAILLES

New Orleans often brings to mind its vibrant creole culture, but there is also a small and prominent Vietnamese American community in Versailles in eastern New Orleans. In an article in New America Media with Sandip Roy, filmmaker and producer of *A Village Called Versailles* Leo Chiang explained that this community came to be as a result of Catholic sponsors who sheltered refugees after the war. Many resettled permanently in New Orleans because the area offered incentives similar to Vietnam, including its location near the shore of the Gulf of Mexico and opportunities for fishing jobs.

Hurricane Katrina devastated New Orleans in 2005, and Versailles was not spared. But as Chiang revealed, Versailles was neglected in the rebuilding process. Even worse, it was selected as the executive area to deposit the debris from the hurricane. Many joined forces in fighting this decision, including the youth of the Vietnamese American community. Chiang's documentary follows the legal battle of the small Vietnamese American community in making sure that they can rebuild Versailles.

1992, the county and the country saw its first Vietnamese immigrant elected into office. Tony Lam served as a city councilman in Westminster. He was a first-wave refugee who eventually became a naturalized citizen and the owner of three successful restaurants.

Besides California, Texas also has a high percentage of Vietnamese immigrants. About 12 percent of Vietnamese immigrants live in Texas, and the highest concentration (74,000) is in the metropolitan area of Houston, Sugar Land, and Baytown. Like Westminster, Houston maintains a vibrant enclave of the Vietnamese diaspora, with Vietnamese-language newspapers, temples, restaurants, stores, and street signs. Vu Thanh Thuy and Duong Phuc own the Vietnamese-language internationally accessible radio station Radio Saigon Houston 900 AM.

The state of Texas also saw the first Vietnamese American to play in the National Football League. Dat Tan Nguyen played college football at Texas A&M University. There, he broke the university's record in number of tackles. He then played for the Dallas Cowboys. He was elected to the College Football Hall of Fame in 2017.

Australia has the second-largest Vietnamese immigrant population (226,000) and Canada is home to the third-largest Vietnamese diaspora population. France has the fourth-largest at 128,000. However, most of the Vietnamese diaspora is in the United States. According to Batalova and Rkasnuam, there were in total 1,259,000 Vietnamese immigrants in the United States in 2012. Of those, most became naturalized citizens. However, the number of Vietnamese people moving to the

HOW VIETNAMESE IMMIGRANTS MADE AMERICA HOME

Former Dallas Cowboy player Dat Tan Nguyen is the child of Vietnamese refugees who escaped Vietnam before the fall of Saigon.

United States has decreased. Only 5 percent of Vietnamese immigrants came to the United States between 2010 and 2017.

Many Vietnamese immigrants and Vietnamese Americans still have close ties to Vietnam. Remittance sent to Vietnam has drastically increased over time, and in 2013, it accounted for 6 percent, or $10.3 billion, of Vietnam's gross domestic product. Furthermore, as Vu mentioned, in 1994, the Clinton administration ended its imposed trade embargo on Vietnam. The United States and Vietnam resumed diplomatic relations the following year.

MYTHS AND FACTS

Myth
All Asians are the same.

Fact
Asian Americans tend to be lumped into one racial group. They are often called simply Asian. Further, the most common assumption is that all Asians are Chinese. However, the Asian identity applies to people from forty-eight different countries. These countries and their people are as distinct from each other as those countries and people of every other continent.

Myth
Asians are an ideal minority that less collectively prosperous minorities should aspire to.

Fact
According to Dr. Uy, the concept of model minority started during the civil rights movement. Anti–civil rights partisans used Asians "as bait to undermine the civil rights movement." In other words, the idea of the model minority shifts the focus away from issues that different ethnic groups are facing and attempting to address.

Regarding the question of Asian success, this stereotype lumps all Asians together and treats them as if they are all the same. Dr. Uy explained that Southeast Asian youths tend to have one of the highest dropout rates among students. In California, Southeast Asians and Pacific Islanders have one of the highest incarceration rates. The model-minority stereotype intentionally masks issues within those communities.

MYTH
Asian women are hypersexual, and Asian men are asexual.

FACT
According to Uy, another stereotype that has historical context is that of the sexualized Asian woman. Due to anti-Asian immigration laws during the early nineteenth century, many Chinese men were not allowed to bring their families into the United States. Such policies had the effect of curtailing the immigrant/first-generation American presence as much as possible. The only females allowed in were prostitutes.

During the Vietnam War, many American soldiers impregnated Vietnamese women and created a new population of Amerasian children. Rape was a weapon of war that Americans used while in Vietnam, so many children were conceived through rape. Some children likely were conceived through consensual relationships.

Despite the reality of which ethnic groups committed which acts, in the United States, the stereotype that lumps all Asians together and then sexualizes Asian women and

(continued on the next page)

MYTHS AND FACTS

(continued from the previous page)

emasculates Asian men still prevails. The stereotype stands in the way of Americans taking responsibility for their actions and for their policies that attempted to establish a particular sexual identity for Asian peoples. The stereotype also stands in the way of accurately defining who has participated in sexual depravity.

FACT SHEET

Countries Where Most of the Vietnamese Diaspora Live
United States
Australia
Canada
France

US States Where Most Vietnamese Americans Live
California
Texas
Washington State
Florida

Notable Vietnamese Americans
Tony Lam was the first Vietnamese American to be elected to political office in the United States.

Viet Thanh Nguyen is a prominent writer. His novel *The Sympathizer* received the Pulitzer Prize for Fiction in 2016.

Dat Tan Nguyen played professional football for the Dallas Cowboys from 1999 to 2005.

Actress Maggie Q is known for her role in the Divergent series.

Jane Luu, an astronomer at MIT, was awarded the prestigious Shaw Prize in Astronomy and the Kavli Prize in Astrophysics in 2012 for her pioneering work studying the Kuiper Belt.

TIMELINE

939 CE Chinese occupation ends, making Vietnam an independent kingdom.

1858 French colonialism officially begins.

1945 Ho Chi Minh declares Vietnam an independent state.

1954 France is defeated in the battle of Dien Bien Phu. The Geneva Accords are signed, ending French claim over Vietnam and dividing the country into North Vietnam and South Vietnam.

1963 Ngo Dinh Diem, president of South Vietnam, is killed.

1964 The Gulf of Tonkin Incident occurs.

1965 The Rolling Thunder campaign begins and severely damages the infrastructure of North Vietnam.

1968 American soldiers commit genocide in My Lai, South Vietnam.

1970 The Vietnamization of the war begins, and the United States withdraws from the war.

1975 President Gerald Ford approves the evacuation of more than one hundred thousand South Vietnamese people to the United States. North Vietnam conquers Saigon, and Congress passes the Indochina Migration and Refugee Assistance Act to fund the resettlement program.

1979 Vietnam invades Cambodia, which exhausts its relationship with China and leads to a temporary Chinese invasion.

1980 Congress passes the Refugee Act of 1980 in response to the refugee crisis.

TIMELINE

1987 Congress passes the Amerasian Homecoming Act to bring forty-six thousand children of American servicemen to the United States

1992 Tony Lam becomes the first Vietnamese immigrant to be elected to office.

1994 The United States ends its trade embargo on Vietnam.

1995 The United States and Vietnam resume their diplomatic relations.

2016 Viet Thanh Nguyen's debut novel, *The Sympathizer*, is awarded the Pulitzer Prize for Fiction.

2017 Dat Tan Nguyen is elected to the College Football Hall of Fame.

GLOSSARY

asylum A legal right to stay in a country, usually granted to people seeking shelter away from war or terrorism in their homeland.

communism A political and economic system in which property is publicly owned and the amount of a financial reward depends on a person's need or ability.

corvée Mandatory labor that citizens must do periodically and as part of their civic duty.

demographic Statistics concerning groups within a population.

diaspora An ethnic group of people from one country that lives outside of the country of origin.

discrimination The act of treating a person or group of people worse than another in order to deprive the badly treated individual or group of equality.

dynasty A group of leaders descended from a single family whose individuals rule over a territory subsequently.

emigration Leaving one's homeland.

enclave An area within a country that is dominated by a specific group.

Hoa Upper-class Vietnamese people of one of three Chinese ethnic groups. Hoa people owned most wealth under South Vietnamese rule.

hypersexual Very sexual; describing a person with little sense of being or ambition outside of sexual expression. Holding such a view about someone is often the result of a stereotype.

immigration Permanently settling in a country that is not

GLOSSARY

one's homeland.

income The money that a government, business, or individual earns by selling goods or services, or in the case of a government, by taxing citizens, goods, and services.

instigated Made an action or event occur.

minority A distinct group of people who are not the majority group.

naturalized citizen A foreign-born person who acquires the citizenship of a given country

permanent resident A person who is admitted to reside in a given country even though that person is not a citizen.

refugees People who are forced to leave their country because of a natural disaster or a political crisis.

remittance Money sent by members of an immigrant community to people in their home country.

self-determined Able to act on free choice.

stereotype A misconception applied to a specific group of people.

strafing Attacking repeatedly.

Viet A member of the Vietnamese ethnic group.

Viet Cong Those in the south of Vietnam who fought for the reunification of Vietnam and who were called Vietnamese Communists.

FOR MORE INFORMATION

VAYLA New Orleans
13235 Chef Menteur Highway, Suite A
New Orleans, LA 70129
(504) 253-6000
Website: http://www.vayla-no.org
Facebook: @VAYLANO
VAYLA is an organization started by the youth of the
    Southeast Asian community in New Orleans in response
    to the obstacles the community faced in rebuilding their
    neighborhood after Hurricane Katrina.

The Vietnam Center and Archive
Texas Tech University
PO Box 41045
Lubbock, TX 79409-1045
(806) 742-9010
Website: https://www.vietnam.ttu.edu
Facebook and Twitter: @vietnamTTU
The Vietnam Center and Archive provides a large database of
    documents about the Vietnam War.

Vietnamese American Civic Association (VACA)
VACA – Hoi Viet My
42 Charles Street
Dorchester, MA 02122
(617) 288-7344
Website: http://www.vaca-boston.org
Vietnamese immigrants founded VACA in 1984 to provide

FOR MORE INFORMATION

new Vietnamese immigrants in the United States with the resources and services they need.

Vietnamese American Studies Center (VASC)
San Francisco State University
1600 Holloway Avenue
EP 103
San Francisco, CA 94132-4252
(415) 338-2698
Website: http://aas.sfsu.edu/content/vietnamese-american
   -studies-center
VASC is part of the Asian American Studies Department at San Francisco State University. Its goal is to address the growing population of Vietnamese Americans.

Vietnamese Association, Toronto (VAT)
1364 Dundas Street West
Toronto, Ontario, M6J 1Y2
Canada
(416) 536-3611
Website: http://www.vatoronto.ca/en
VAT is a volunteer-based organization that offers many services to the Vietnamese Canadian community.

Vietnamese Canadian Federation (VCF)
2476 Regatta Avenue
Ottawa, ON K2J 5V6
Canada

(780) 708-0876
Website: http://vietfederation.ca/en
VCF is a community-based national organization in Canada.

Viet Stories: Vietnamese American Oral History Project
University of California, Irvine
Department of Asian American Studies
3110 Humanities Gateway
Irvine, CA 92697-6955
Website: http://sites.uci.edu/vaohp
Facebook: @VAOHP
This nonprofit organization collects the oral histories of the first-generation Vietnamese immigrants and preserves them for future generations.

FOR FURTHER READING

Boyle, Brenda M, and Jeehyun Lim. *Looking Back on the Vietnam War: Twenty-First Century Perspectives*. New Brunswick, NJ: Rutgers University Press, 2016.

Chorlian, Meg. *The New Face of Immigration*. Peterborough, NH: Cobblestone, 2013.

Howell, Sara. *Refugees* (The American Mosaic: Immigration Today). New York, NY: Rosen Publishing, 2015.

Kingston, Anna. *Respecting the Contributions of Asian Americans* (Stop Bullying Now!) New York, NY: Rosen Publishing, 2013.

Lee, Jennifer, and Min Zhou. *The Asian American Achievement Paradox*. New York, NY: Russell Sage Foundation, 2015.

Marciano, John D. *The American War in Vietnam: Crime or Commemoration?* New York, NY: Monthly Review Press, 2016.

Rose, Simon. *The Vietnam War 1954–1975*. New York, NY: AV2 by Weigl, 2014.

Seah, Audrey, Charissa M. Nair, Debbie Nevins, and Charles Piddock. *Vietnam*. New York, NY: Benchmark Books, 2015.

Sirvaitis, Karen. *The Asian Pacific American Experience*. Brookfield, CT: Twenty-First Century Books, 2014.

Skrypuch, Marsha Forchuk, Brian Deines, and Tuan Ho. *Adrift at Sea: A Vietnamese Boy's Story of Survival*. Toronto, ON: Pajama Press, 2016.

BIBLIOGRAPHY

Avakian, Monique. *Atlas of Asian-American History.* New York, NY: Checkmark Books, 2002.

Batalova, Jeanne, and Hataipreuk Rkasnuam. "Vietnamese Immigrants in the United States." Migration Policy Institute, August 25, 2014. http://www.migrationpolicy.org/article/vietnamese-immigrants-united-states-2.

Caputo, Philip. *10,000 Days of Thunder: A History of the Vietnam War.* New York, NY: Atheneum Books for Young Readers, 2005.

CBC News. "Kim Thuy's Novel *Ru* Draws on Refugee Past." March 19, 2012. http://www.cbc.ca/news/entertainment/kim-thuy-s-novel-ru-draws-on-refugee-past-1.1279940.

CBC Radio. "The Vietnam War: Canada's Role, Part Two: The Boat People." April 30, 2015. http://www.cbc.ca/radio/rewind/the-vietnam-war-canada-s-role-part-two-the-boat-people-1.3048026.

Chan, Sucheng. *Asian Americans: An Interpretive History.* New York, NY: Twayne Publishers, 1991.

Cherenfant, Sabine (interviewer), and Phitsamay Sychitkokhong Uy (interviewee). "2017 Interview: Issues That Vietnamese Americans Face." August 25, 2017.

Do, Anh. "Vietnamese Refugees Began New Lives in Camp Pendleton's 1975 'Tent City.'" *Los Angeles Times*, April 29, 2015. http://graphics.latimes.com/tent-city.

Do, Anh, and Christopher Goffard. "Orange County Home to Third-Largest Asian American Population in U.S." *Los Angeles Times*, July 13, 2014. http://www.latimes.com

BIBLIOGRAPHY

/local/orangecounty/la-me-asian-oc-20140714-story.html.

Embassy of the Socialist Republic of Vietnam in the United Kingdom. "Population and Ethnics." Accessed August 25, 2017. http://www.vietnamembassy.org.uk/population.html.

Flakus, Greg. "Houston's Vietnamese-Language Radio Binds Community." VOA, October 10, 2016. https://www.voanews.com/a/houston-vietnamese-language-radio-binds-community/3543759.html.

Gall, Timothy L., and Jeneen Hobb. *Worldmark Encyclopedia of Cultures and Daily Life Volume 4: Asia and Oceana.* Farmington Hills, MI: Gale, 2009.

Gandhi, Lakshmi. "Former Dallas Cowboy Dat Nguyen to Be Inducted to College Football Hall of Fame." NBC News, January 10, 2017. https://www.nbcnews.com/news/asian-america/former-dallas-cowboy-dat-nguyen-be-inducted-college-football-hall-n705206.

Grad, Shelby. "As Trump Bans Syrian Refugees, a Look Back at When California Welcomed 50,000 Displaced People." *Los Angeles Times*, January 28, 2017. http://www.latimes.com/local/lanow/la-me-trump-refugees-camp-pendleton-retrospective-20170128-story.html.

Lamb, David. "Children of the Vietnam War." *Smithsonian Magazine*, June 2009. http://www.smithsonianmag.com/travel/children-of-the-vietnam-war-131207347.

Morgan, Ted. *Valley of Death: The Tragedy at Dien Bien Phu* that Led America into the Vietnam War. New York, NY: Random House, 2010.

Murray, Stuart. *Eyewitness: Vietnam War*. New York, NY: DK Publishing, 2017.

Mydans, Seth. "A Vietnamese-American Becomes a Political First." *New York Times*, November 16, 1992. http://www.nytimes.com/1992/11/16/us/a-vietnamese-american-becomes-a-political-first.html.

Ngo, Anh. "A Case Study of the Vietnamese in Toronto: Contesting Representations of the Vietnamese in Canadian Social Work Literature." *Refuge* 32, no. 2 (2016). https://refuge.journals.yorku.ca/index.php/refuge/article/view/40262.

Perrin, Linda. *Coming to America: Immigrants from the Far East*. New York, NY: Delacorte Press, 1980.

Pham, Michelle. "Wrestler Carol Huynh Brought Home Olympic Bronze. Was It Good Enough?" *Vancouver Observer*, September 4, 2012. http://www.vancouverobserver.com/olympics/wrestler-carol-huynh-brought-home-olympic-bronze-was-it-good-enough.

Salamon, Julie. "Television Review; When Those Orphaned by War Return to Vietnam." *New York Times*, December 22, 2001. http://www.nytimes.com/2001/12/22/arts/television-review-when-those-orphaned-by-war-return-to-vietnam.html.

Senate of Canada. "Senator Thanh Hai Ngo." Accessed September 11, 2017. https://sencanada.ca/en/senators/ngo-thanh-hai.

BIBLIOGRAPHY

Stanford University. "History and Backround of Communism." Accessed August 30, 2017. https://cs.stanford.edu/people/eroberts/cs201/projects/communism-computing-china/index.html.

Turley, William S. *The Second Indochina War: A Concise Political and Military History*. Plymouth, UK: Rowman & Littlefield Publishers, 2009.

Vu, Hong Lien, and Peter D. Sharrock. *Descending Dragon, Rising Tiger: A History of Vietnam*. London, UK: Reaktion Books, 2014.

INDEX

A
Agent Orange, 42
Amerasian Homecoming Act, 8–9, 33, 50
animism, 45
asylum, 8, 48
Australia, 8, 29, 45, 57

B
Bao Dai, 20
boat people, 8, 43–44
Buddhism, 13–14, 20, 26, 45

C
California, 39–40, 53–57
Cambodia, 20, 26, 32, 37, 43, 45
Canada, 8, 20, 45, 48–49, 57
Caodaism, 13
Catholicism, 13, 20, 37, 40–41, 45, 56
Celler, Emanuel, 46
Champa Empire, 11, 30
Chiang, Leo, 56
China, 7, 11, 13–14, 16, 24–25, 29, 43
communism, 7–8, 16, 19–20, 22, 24, 26, 36, 43
Confucianism, 13–14
corvée, 16
coup, 26–27
culture shock, 9

D
Demilitarized Zone, 7, 19
Diem, Ngo Dinh, 7, 20, 24, 26–27
Dien Bien Phu, Battle of, 19
discrimination, 9, 33, 36, 51
dynasties, 7, 14, 30

E
education, 8–9, 16, 37, 41, 52, 54
Eisenhower, Dwight, 20
embargo, 59
emperors, 14, 16, 20
enclave, 53–54, 57
Engels, Friedrich, 22, 24

F
farming, 8, 13, 43
First Indochina War, 7, 17, 19–20
food, 13, 57
football, 57
Ford, Gerald, 36
France, 7–8, 13, 16–17, 19–20, 24, 29, 45, 57

INDEX

G
Geneva Accords, 7, 19–21, 25–26
genocide, 30
Giap, Vo Nguyen, 19
Guam, 39
Gulf of Tonkin Incident, 8, 27
Gulf of Tonkin Resolution, 27, 32

H
Hart, Philip, 46
herbicides, 8, 29, 42–43
Hmong people, 11, 44–45
Hoa people, 11, 43
Ho Chi Minh Trail, 26
Houston (Texas), 57

I
Immigration and Nationality Act of 1965, 46
income, 52
Indochina Migration and Refugee Assistance Act, 46
Indochinese Parole Programs, 47–48
Islam, 13
isolation, 53

J
Johnson, Lyndon B., 27, 31

K
Katrina, Hurricane, 56
Korean War, 24

L
Lam, Tony, 37, 57
language barrier, 8, 52, 54
Laos, 20, 26, 32, 37, 45
Louisiana, 53, 56

M
Malaysia, 44
Marshall, George Catlett, 24
Marshall Plan, 24
Marx, Karl, 22, 24
matriarchal society, 13
McCarran-Walter Act, 36, 46
migration within Vietnam, 7, 20, 25
Minh, Ho Chi, 7, 17, 19–20, 26
misdiagnoses, 54
multigenerational households, 52
My Lai massacre, 30

N

National Liberation Front (Viet Cong), 26, 29–30, 32, 48
naturalized citizen, 57
Ngai people, 11, 13
Nguyen, Dat Tan, 57
Nhu, Ngo Dinh, 20, 26–27
Nixon, Richard, 31–32, 36

O

Operation Babylift, 33–34
Operation Freewind, 34
Orange County (California), 53–57

P

patriarchal society, 13
Pendleton, Camp, 37, 40
permanent resident, 48
Pham, Andrew X., 45
Philippines, 29, 44
pho, 13
Phuc, Duong, 57
piracy, 8, 44
post-traumatic stress disorder (PTSD), 54
prisoners of war, 9

Q

quoc ngu, 16

R

Radio Saigon Houston, 57
receiving camps, 8, 39–40
Refugee Act of 1980, 47–48
remittances, 59
rice, 13
Rolling Thunder, 8, 27, 29, 31
Russia, 24–25, 29

S

Search and Destroy, 29–30, 32
secondary migration, 53–54
Second Indochina War
  casualties, 8, 30, 32–34
  evacuation, 33–34
  first phase, 26–27
  motivation for, 7–8, 19–21, 24
  refugee crisis, 8, 22, 36–37
  second phase, 27, 29–30
  tactics, 8, 27, 29–30, 32
  third phase, 30–32
  US opposition to, 30–31
soccer, 13

INDEX

South China Sea, 13–14
Special Parole Program of 1975, 47–48
sponsorship, 8, 39–41, 48–49, 56
strafing, 27

T
Taoism, 13
tent cities, 37, 40–41, 54
Tet Offensive, 30, 32
Texas, 53, 57
Thailand, 26, 29, 44
Thuy, Vu Thanh, 57
Truman, Harry, 24
Trung sisters, 14

U
United Nations High Commissioner for Refugees, 48
United States Catholic Conference, 40–41
Uy, Phitsamay, 52, 54

V
Versailles, Louisiana, 56
Viet Minh, 17, 19–20, 26
Vietnam
  culture, 13–14
  ethnic groups, 11, 13
  French control, 7, 10, 16–17, 19, 24
  geography, 11
  independence, 7, 19–21
  postwar, 8, 41–43, 59
  precolonial history, 7, 11, 14
  religions, 13
  US intervention in, 7–8, 19–21, 24, 26
Vietnamese immigration
  first wave, 8, 34, 36–37, 39–41, 46–47, 52, 57
  second wave, 8, 43–50, 52
  third wave, 8–9, 33, 50
  twenty-first-century, 57, 59
Vietnamese language, 11, 13, 16, 54, 57
VOLAG, 40–41

W
Westminster (California), 53–55, 57
Westmoreland, William C., 29

ABOUT THE AUTHOR

Sabine Cherenfant moved to the United States when she was fourteen years old. She grew up experiencing the struggles of assimilating and resettling. In 2012, she published a research paper on how to successfully create a diversity department in universities and colleges to address equity issues in post-secondary institutions. Cherenfant lives in New Jersey.

PHOTO CREDITS

Cover, p. 3 Judy Bellah/Lonely Planet Images/Getty Images; p. 6 Three Lions/Hulton Archive/Getty Images; pp. 10, 22, 38, 51 Konstantin L/Shutterstock.com (pamphlet), Rigamondis/Shutterstock.com (fingerprint), ducu59us/Shutterstock.com (USA logo); p. 12 Indochina studio/Shutterstock.com; pp. 15, 17 Pictures from History/Bridgeman Images; pp. 18, 23, 25 Bettmann/Getty Images; p. 28 Keystone/Hulton Archive/Getty Images; pp. 31, 39, 42, 47 © AP Images; pp. 34–35 Frank Lennon/Toronto Star/Getty Images; p. 44 Fred Ihrt/LightRocket/Getty Images; p. 49 Dirck Halstead/Hulton Archive/Getty Images; p. 53 RosaIreneBetancourt 12/Alamy Stock Photo; p. 55 ullstein bild/Getty Images; pp. 58–59 Jeff Gross/Getty Images; cover and interior pages Alexander Ryabintsev/Shutterstock.com (passport stamps); interior pages Sergiy Palamarchuk/Shutterstock.com (US visa), Ollyy/Shutterstock.com (portraits collage).

Design: Nelson Sá; Layout: Nicole Russo-Duca; Photo Researcher: Bruce Donnola